Contents

List of Illustrations

Abstract

Kenya, Ethiopia, and South Sudan recently embarked on a $25 billion oil production project in Lamu, Kenya. Otherwise known as the Lamu-South-Sudan-Ethiopia-Transport-Corridor (LAPSSET) project, it is expected to bring these nations and others throughout East Africa out of poverty and transform their social status from economic and social despair to economic prosperity. The LAPSSET project will include a 32 berth mega port, a railway, an oil pipeline, a highway, and a fiber optic network. They key component to the entire project is the oil pipeline. But the construction and ultimate uninterrupted use of the oil pipeline is facing many security threats. Al-Shabaab in Somalia, armed rebel groups, and armed militia in South Sudan pose the greatest security challenges to the oil pipeline. This threat directly opposes U.S. AFRICA COMMAND's (U.S. AFRICOM) strategic and operational goals of security and stability throughout the East African region. Consequently, U.S. AFRICOM must immediately engage these nations to help put in place security measures to mitigate attack from these groups.

INTRODUCTION

> I have no doubt that this day will go down in history as one of the defining moments – when we made a major stride to connect our people to the many socio-economic opportunities that lie ahead . . . I am proud to say this is one of the biggest projects we are carrying out in Africa.
>
> -Mwai Kibaki

The African nations of Kenya, South Sudan, and Ethiopia recently broke ground on one of the most ambitious projects ever undertaken on the African continent; on March 2, 2012 work officially began on the Lamu-Port-South-Sudan-Ethiopia-Transport-Corridor (LAPSSET) project.[1] The $25 billion project, which includes a 32 berth mega port, a railway, an oil pipeline, a highway, and a fiber optic network, shoulders the economic hope and fortune for millions of Africans living in the region. If all goes according to plan, the LAPSSET project is expected to become the leading trade and development center for East Africa, potentially bringing millions of Africans out of destitute poverty.[2]

Despite the enthusiasm from government leaders and the civilian population, great anxiety exists. The porous security environment that envelops the East African region creates an opportunity for a variety of rebel groups, armed militia, and terrorists to physically destroy elements of the LAPSSET project. Of these elements, the most vulnerable is the oil pipeline, which is scheduled to pass through Kenya and South Sudan. A successful attack on the pipeline would disrupt and potentially destroy the economic fortune so many Africans are counting on. To help bring economic prosperity to East Africa, United States Africa

---

[1] Lamu Port Project Launched for South Sudan and Ethiopia, British Broadcasting Corporation (BBC) News Africa, last modified March 2, 2012, http://www.bbc.co.uk/news/world-africa-17231889
[2] African Leaders Launch "Super Port" Project, Al Jazeera, last modified March 2, 2012, http://www.aljazeera.com/news/africa/2012/03/20123283443196129.html

1

Command (U.S. AFRICOM) must work with Kenya and South Sudan to institute security measures along the Lamu oil pipeline to mitigate threats from terrorist attacks.

BACKGROUND

In the early part of the 20th century, Sudan was part of Egypt. In 1956, during a decade when most African nations achieved independence from their European colonizers, Sudan capitalized on the momentum and seceded from Egypt. But within the new nation of Sudan, there were strong desires to establish an independent South Sudan; these citizens saw themselves as distinct from their northern countrymen. After decades of fighting and debate, South Sudan achieved its independence in July 2011. One of the most significant decisions the new government made was to stop oil exportation north through the Greater Nile Oil Pipeline to the Red Sea via Sudan. (See Figure 1.)

Figure 1[3]
Greater Nile Oil Pipeline

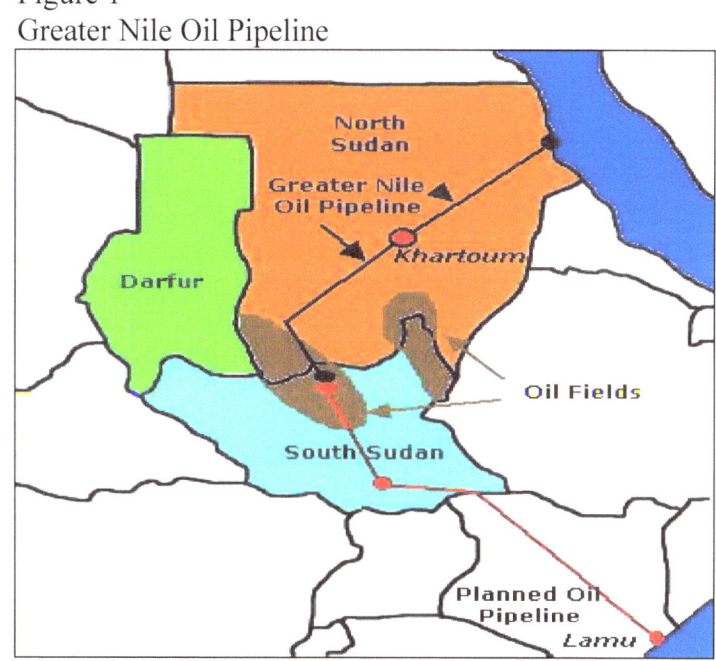

[3] Ole Nielsen, "Slitting Sudan Oil," *Nielsen Blog, November 16, 2010,*
http://my.opera.com/nielsol/blog/2010/11/16/splitting-sudan-and-oil

This decision negatively impacted the Sudanese economy, which relied heavily on oil exportation as a source of income for the nation. The worth of Sudanese oil exports in 1999 was valued at $275.9 million and increased to $8,418.5 million in 2007.[4] The Sudanese had relied heavily on this source of income to fund projects within the country. In the fall of 2011, South Sudan made the decision to cut off oil exportation to Sudan creating a vacuum the Sudanese economy is still trying to fill. The Sudanese government and its citizens were angered by the oil decision, and it became the primary source of the tense relationship between the two nations. While South Sudan has tried to restart the exportation of this precious resource to Sudan, Kenya and Ethiopia came forth with a better alternative.

Kenya and Ethiopia agreed to partner with South Sudan to contribute to the success of the LAPSSET project. These nations agreed to initially fund beginning portions of the project which will eventually cost $25 billion and include the following elements: a 32 berth mega port in Lamu, Kenya, a 1710 kilometer (km) railway connecting Kenya and Ethiopia, a 2,240 km oil pipeline connecting the oil fields in South Sudan to the refineries in Lamu, a 880 km highway linking Lamu to South Sudan and Ethiopia, and finally, a fiber-optic network (See figure 2.).[5] As part of the agreement to begin construction of the oil pipeline, which will be able to export 500,000 barrels of crude oil per day, South Sudan agreed to pay for this element of the project, which will make them responsible for coordinating security measures, a task they are ill-prepared to assume.[6]

---

[4] Hassan Ali Gadkarim, "Oil, Peace and Development: The Sudanese Impasse," Chr. Michelsen Institute, last modified 2010, http://www.cmi.no/publications/file/3793-oil-peace-and-development-the-sudanese-impasse.pdf
[5] Dennis Mayeku, Lamu Port and LAPSSET Construction Project Commenced, Open Book, last modified March 10, 2012, http://www.openbook.co.ke/2012/lamu-port-and-lapsset-construction-project-commenced.html
[6] LAPSSET Corridor And New Lamu Port Feasibility Study and Master Plans Report-Volume Three: LAPSSET Corridor Master Plan and Development Plan, last modified May 2011, http://www.nigrizia.it/public/PDF%20e%20DOCUMENTI/lapsset-executive-summary.pdf

Figure 2[7]
LAPSSET oil pipeline, highway, and railway

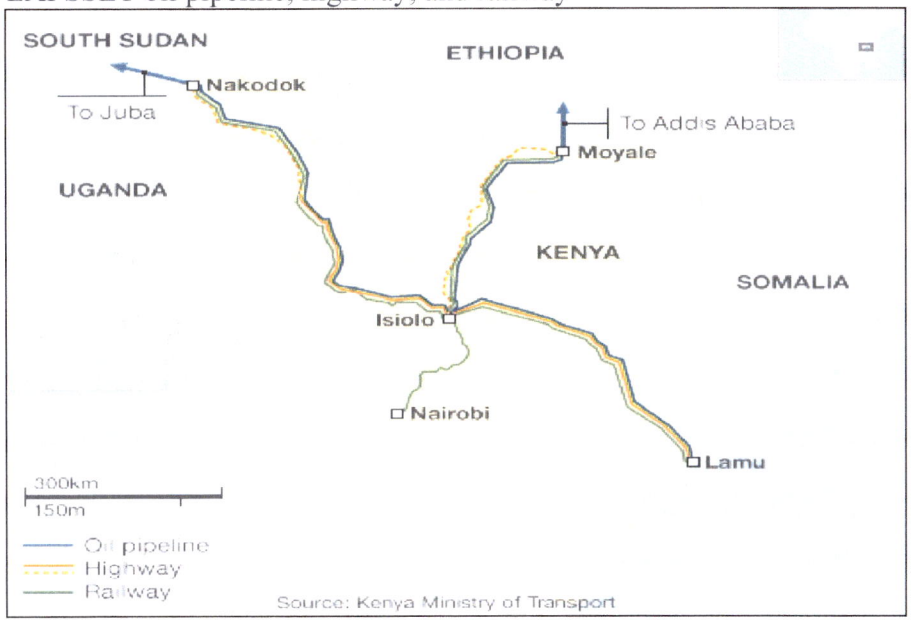

THREATS AND CHALLENGES

On an international level, terrorists, rebel groups, and militia have historically viewed

the oil industry as a target. Though the number of attacks against the oil industry fluctuated

over the decades, the past 30 years have seen an uptick around the world in terrorist groups,

armed rebel groups, and armed militia targeting oil infrastructure. In recent years, direct

attacks against oil infrastructure have become more commonplace. From 1999-2000, various

countries in Latin America experienced 393 oil pipeline attacks.[8] In October 2002, terrorists

conducted a suicide attack on the French supertanker *Limburg* off the coast of Yemen,

resulting in 90,000 barrels of oil spilled, one death, and 17 injuries, and the negative

economic repercussions of oil lost to the global market.[9] From 2003-2006, Shell Oil

---

[7] Lamu Port Project Launched for South Sudan and Ethiopia, BBC News Africa, 2.

[8] Robert Rapier, Oil Infrastructure and Terrorism Part II, Consumer Energy Report, last modified October 6, 2010, http://www.consumerenergyreport.com/2010/10/06/oil-infrastructure-and-terrorism-part-ii

[9] U.S. Government Accountability Office (GAO), *Maritime Security, Federal Efforts Needed to Address Challenges in Preventing and Responding to Terrorist Attacks on Energy Commodity Tankers, 2007 (Washington, DC: GPO, 2007),* 7.

Company officially documented seven major incidents from rebel groups targeting its oil production business in Nigeria.[10] These incidents ranged from kidnappings of oil workers to entire oil facilities being shut down.[11] The most damaging incident occurred in December 2005 when a major Nigerian oil pipeline was destroyed by terrorists, forcing Shell officials to delay crude oil shipments from Nigeria. This delay resulted in the loss of thousands of barrels of crude oil a day and millions of dollars lost to the Nigerian economy.[12]

In September 2007 when a Mexican rebel group, possibly linked to the Popular Revolutionary Army, used bombs to blow up six oil and natural gas pipelines in Veracruz and Tlaxcala states, it caused widespread damage and propagating fears of more politically motivated attacks.[13] In March of 2012, the Cano Limon oil pipeline in Colombia was attacked and portions of it destroyed by leftist guerrillas.[14] This attack was the 15th attack against this pipeline in 2012.[15] These attacks resulted in a significant decrease in oil exportation revenue, negatively impacting the Colombian economy.

The Lamu oil pipeline will not be immune from similar terrorist attacks. If nothing is done to prevent these attacks and they happen, if even on an infrequent basis, the economies of Kenya and South Sudan will continue to suffer. In fact, the threat to the Lamu oil pipeline is greater than to other pipelines located throughout the world. For years, East Africa, where

---

[10] Breane Coble, Shell's Corporate Social Responsibility in the Niger Delta, last modified June 1, 2007, http://www.richmond.ac.uk/cms/pdfs/CobleBrief.pdf
[11] Ibid.
[12] Ibid.
[13] Reed Johnson, "6 Pipelines Blown Up In Mexico," *LA Times*, September 11, 2007, http://articles.latimes.com/2007/sep/11/world/fg-pipelines11
[14] Colombia's Cano Limon Pipeline Shut Down After New Rebel Attack, Fox Business, last modified March 20, 2012, http://www.foxbusiness.com/news/2012/03/20/colombias-cano-limon-pipeline-shut-down-after-new-rebel-attack/
[15] Rapier, Oil Infrastructure and Terrorism Part II, 5.

Kenya and South Sudan are positioned, has been synonymous with terms like insecurity, instability, and failed states. The Failed State Index, collaboratively produced by Foreign Policy magazine and The Fund for Peace, has ranked Kenya and South Sudan in the top 20 on its list of failed states since 2009.[16] The primary drivers that encourage insecurity and instability are Al-Shabaab in Somalia and armed rebel groups and armed militia operating in South Sudan. Each group directly threatens the security of the Lamu oil pipeline. If U.S. AFRICOM does not assist Kenya and South Sudan institute security measures along the oil pipeline to mitigate attacks from either of the aforementioned groups, then the economic prosperity opportunities the LAPSSET project is expected to bring will collapse.

Al-Shabaab

Al-Shabaab has long been an impediment to establishing peace in not only Somalia, but throughout East Africa. Their recent rhetoric is pointing to a more regional approach in carrying out their goal of Islamist jihad against western capitalism and its sympathizers. Established as a militant wing of the Islamist Court Union in 2004, Al-Shabaab fought for influence and control of central and southern Somalia, and specifically in the national capital of Mogadishu.[17] Since that time, Al-Shabaab experienced gains and setbacks. Currently, there is debate as to exactly how capable the organization is in executing attacks, especially expeditionary attacks across national borders. While this debate will undoubtedly continue, two points are of grave concern for U.S. AFRICOM, Kenya, and South Sudan that make Al-

---

[16] The Failed States Index, Foreign Policy, last modified May 1, 2012,
http://www.foreignpolicy.com/articles/2011/06/17/2011_failed_states_index_interactive_map_and_rankings
From 2009-2011, Somalia has been ranked as the highest ranking failed state in the world, Sudan has ranked third in each of the last three years and Kenya ranked 13th in 2009 and 2010 but fell to 16th in the 2011 rankings.
[17] Geoffrey B. Kambere, "Countering Al-Shabaab: A Case to Minimize Transnational Terrorist Threats Against Uganda" (Master of Science thesis, Naval Post Graduate School, 2011), 4, DTIC (ADA 556426).

Shabaab an expeditionary organization capable of conducting terrorist acts on a transnational level.

First, on February 9, 2012, Al-Qaeda and Al-Shabaab jointly announced their formal alliance.[18] This partnership raised the concerns of U.S. AFRICOM's Commander, General Carter Ham, to the point where he states in the 2012 U.S. AFRICOM posture statement that countering terrorism, specifically Al-Qaeda and Al-Shabaab, is a top priority for his Command.[19] His concern is not overblown, as several jihadi theorists expressed their concern of Al-Qaeda desiring to strike oil targets through U.S. AFRICOM's area of responsibility.[20] As David Anderson and Michael Mihalka state in "Is the Sky Falling? Energy Security and Transnational Terrorism", for Al-Qaeda and Al-Shabaab to attain their Islamic caliphate by 2020, they must accomplish three specific tasks.[21] First, which was already completed, they must awake the Muslim masses through an eye opening attack, i.e. the World Trade Center attack on September 11, 2011. Second, they must deprive the west of energy and deny "proxy regimes" oil revenue. Finally, economic warfare must be waged against the west, including burning oil. A key target of opportunity is the Lamu oil pipeline which fits neatly into Al-Qaeda's and Al-Shabaab's target matrix. Realizing that Al-Shabaab poses a significant threat to the oil pipeline, Kenya took action to try and nullify Al-Shabaab's physical attack capabilities, but they only exacerbated the conflict.

---

[18] Rapier, Oil Infrastructure and Terrorism Part II, 4.
[19] GEN Carter Ham 2012 U.S. AFRICOM Posture Statement, http://www.africom.mil/fetchBinary.asp?pdfID=20120301102747.
[20] David Anderson and Michael Mihalka, Is the Sky Falling? Energy Security and Transnational Terrorism, Center for Contemporary Conflict, 1.
[21] Ibid.

In October 2011, Kenya deployed sections of their military forces into Somalia in an attempt to establish a peaceful Somalia and defeat Al-Shabaab forces.[22] As Kenyan Army and Air Forces north of the border clashed against Al-Shabaab fighters, Al-Shabaab vowed payback. The group claimed that "Kenyan military intervention was rapidly rolling down a path towards ignominious end endured by all previous invaders."[23] Moreover, as Kenyan military response was unrelenting, Al-Shabaab vowed revenge against Kenya; the possibility of a broad conflict within Kenyan national borders was increased.[24] Additional rhetoric by Al-Shabaab left little doubt that they will one day attempt to attack Kenya where it would hurt them most.

By interpreting this information, one can deduce that the Lamu oil pipeline could be a potential target for attack from Al-Shabaab terrorists. The strategic, operational, and tactical components of Al-Qaeda achieving its grand vision of the world align nicely with the oil pipeline. A successful attack on the pipeline would serve the terrorist's overall international strategic objectives as well as accomplish localized goals of promoting regional instability in East Africa. For those who believe that Al-Shabaab is only capable of executing attacks inside Somali borders, they need to look no further than attacks the organization conducted at targets in Kenya, specifically in the capital city of Nairobi in late October 2011.[25] These attacks demonstrate that even if Al-Shabaab has been weakened within their home nation, it still possesses the capability, capacity, and motivation to carry out attacks in places away

[22] Kenyan Troops Kill 60 Al-Shabaab Fighters in Somalia, BBC News Africa, last modified January 7, 2012, http://www.bbc.co.uk/news/world-africa-16455039.
[23] Ibid.
[24] Mustafa Abdi, "Al-Shabab," *New York Times*, October 17, 2011, http://topics.nytimes.com/top/reference/timestopics/organizations/s/al-shabab/index.html
[25] Catherine Herridge, Deadly Attacks Show Al-Shabaab Expanding Its Reach, With Potential for US Targets, Fox News, last modified October 24, 2011, http://www.foxnews.com/world/2011/10/24/deadly-attacks-show-al-shabaab-expanding-its-reach-with-potential-for-us/

from their home base. And now that an official alliance has been garnered by them and Al-Qaeda, presumably, Al-Shabaab has access to a much larger network of resources such as intelligence, personnel, weapons, and communications to continue their aggressive actions. U.S. AFRICOM must realize that the Lamu oil pipeline could serve as the perfect target not only in retaliation for Kenyan aggression, but against Kenyan as well as South Sudanese allegiance to western capitalistic ideals and stances on economic development. Unfortunately for U.S. AFRICOM, the pipeline security problem is more complicated than just trying to minimize an attack from Al-Shabaab, it must also take into account a potential attack from armed rebel groups and armed militia in South Sudan.

Armed Rebel Groups and Armed Militia

In a nation like South Sudan where security is less than optimal and disenfranchisement runs rampant, the presence of armed rebel groups and armed militia is commonplace. Constantly shifting alliances among the rebel groups and militias make it extremely difficult to determine agendas and motivations for the fighting. Additionally, there has been and continues to be a sense of impropriety between government officials and rebels and militia. For years, armed rebel groups and armed militia have been allegedly connected to a multitude of high ranking government officials within the Sudanese and South Sudanese government. In this highly dynamic relationship between official governments and "under the table" rebel groups and militia, one thing is for certain, that for as long as there is animosity and conflict between Sudan and South Sudan, the exploitation of armed rebel groups and armed militia will be maximized. While the two governments try and settle their differences peacefully, armed attacks have occurred and both sides have accused the other of arming rebel groups and militia to try and gain leverage over the other. The primary

roadblock to peace is the disputed Heglig oil region along the border where both countries

claim national sovereignty. (See Figure 3.)

Figure 3[26]
Heglig Oil Fields

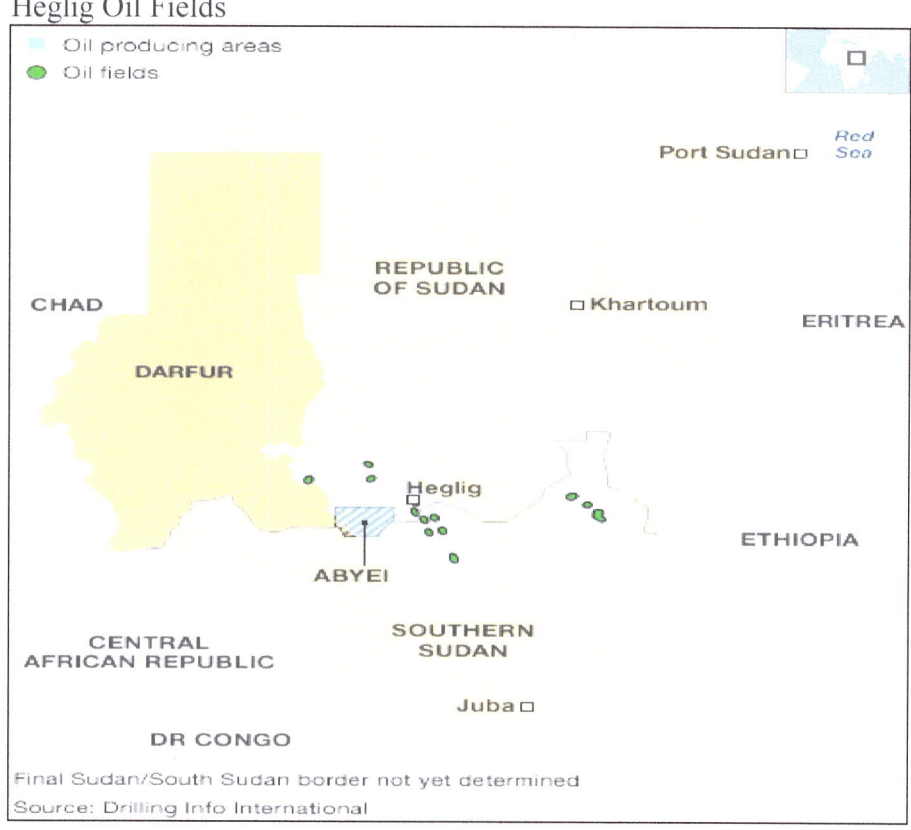

The majority of the oil producing region lies within the national boundaries of South

Sudan. As mentioned earlier, a root of conflict between Sudan and South Sudan is that

Sudan no longer has access to the riches these oil fields produce. To try and gain negotiating

leverage, Sudan has purportedly used armed rebel groups and armed militia to disrupt any

attempt to begin, conduct, and complete construction of the Lamu oil pipeline in the hope of

redirecting oil back to the north. The South Sudan Liberation Army (SSLA) and the South

[26] South Sudan To Withdraw Troops from Heglig Oil Field, BBC News Africa, last modified April 20, 2012, http://www.bbc.co.uk/news/world-africa-17787142

Sudan Democratic Army (SSDA), both allegedly supported by Sudan in terms of money, logistics, and weapons, threatened to attack the Lamu oil pipeline in January 2012.[27] Whatever their motivations, the fact remains that these two organizations have warned any oil company and western supporting nations that any attempt to begin construction of the oil pipeline will be met with violence.[28] Both groups are serious threats. To further muddle matters, South Sudan witnessed numerous renegade militias, composed of high level Sudan's People Liberation Army (SPLA) defectors make aggressive statements regarding their unhappiness about the way in which the Lamu oil pipeline deal was reached. The SPLA has openly stated that the oil pipeline is in jeopardy unless the South Sudanese government is willing to hear their side of the story.[29] Even if South Sudan listens, there is no guarantee that both sides would come to an agreement. With shifting alliances and the desire to advance personal interests at the expense of regional stability and peace, these rebel groups and armed militia pose a significant threat to the security of the Lamu oil pipeline. Not only must U.S. AFRICOM, Kenya, and South Sudan confront the challenges posed by these various groups, they must also fight against a more stable opponent, the challenging geography of the region through which the Lamu oil pipeline will be built.

Additional Challenges

Given the demonstrated need for security, the length of the Lamu oil pipeline, often running through desolate and rural countryside, makes it challenging for Kenya and South

---

[27] South Sudan's Rebel Groups Threatened To Prevent The Construction of New Oil Pipeline; Warned "Theaters of War", South Sudan News Agency, last modified January 25, 2012, http://www.southsudannewsagency.com/news/press-releases/south-sudans-rebel-groups-threatened-to-prevent-the-construction-of-new-oil-pipeline-warned-theaters-of-war

[28] Ibid.

[29] Jens Pedersen, South Sudan: Nation Building Through a Pipeline?, Michelsen Institute, last modified April 2012, http://www.cmi.no/sudan/resources.cfm?id=918-south-sudan-nationbuilding-through-a-pipeline

Sudan to provide security. The majority of the pipeline will run through Kenya, with a smaller portion passing through South Sudan. Working its way north from Lamu, the oil pipeline will pass through Kenyan towns such as Bura, Garissa, Isiolo, and Lokichogio before passing into South Sudan. Isiolo is the most populated of these cities with 73,000 citizens as of 2011.[30] Much of the Kenyan countryside is barren and mountainous, making it difficult to institute security measures along the route. When the oil pipeline passes into South Sudanese territory, the geography remains a challenge. The pipeline passes through the remote town of Torit before making its way north to Juba and ultimately into the oil fields north of the city. (See figure 4.)

Figure 4[31]
Proposed Lamu Oil Pipeline Route

---

[30] Food and Medical Aid for 73,000 People, Malteser International, last modified April 11, 2012, http://www.malteser-international.org/en/home/where-we-help/africa/kenya/relief-reconstruction rehabilitations/food-and-medical-aid-for-73000-people.html
[31] Huge Lamu Port Project Launched for South Sudan and Ethiopia, Word Press, last modified March 11, 2012, http://seeker401.wordpress.com/2012/03/11/massive-lamu-port-project-launched-for-south-sudan-and-ethiopia/

Border security is another challenge. The security situation along the Kenya-South Sudan border resembles the American Wild West. Terrorists and bands of disenfranchised youth roam the area and pass from one nation to another without having to pass through border checkpoints. This lack of border security, coupled with the heavy presence of small arms and light weapons, as well as ample ammunition in the vicinity of the border region, make it a high threat area.[32] Contributing to this lack of border control have been numerous violent attacks along the border making it a very unstable area. Al-Shabaab conducted these attacks using grenades, improvised explosive devices, kidnappings, and bombs. They proved Kenya cannot secure its side of the border (neither can Somalia) which affords them the ability to carry out attacks in Kenyan territory whenever and however they wish. This makes a pending attack on the Lamu oil pipeline a real possibility in the future. This environment does not bode well for security as the pipeline will pass close to the Somali border, affording Al-Shabaab terrorists an attractive target for attack.

Though Juba is the capital of South Sudan and one would think that the capital city of a nation would have adequate security to protect the pipeline as it passes through, that is far from the case. The U.S. Department of State published a crime and safety report for Juba in 2011 which warned that the overall crime and safety situation in Juba is ripe with crime threats, poor road safety, high potential for political violence, and a threat for international and transnational terrorism.[33] Not much has changed in the early months of 2012, especially given the recent violence stemming from the disputed Heglig oil fields in the region. Finally,

[32] Simon Simonse, Human Security in the Borderlands of Sudan, Uganda, and Kenya, IKV Pax Christi, last modified July 2011, http://www.ikvpaxchristi.nl/files/Documenten/afrika/IKV%20Pax%20Christi%20Human%20security%20in%0the%20borderlands%20of%20Sudan%20Uganda%20and%20Kenya.pdf

[33] U.S. Department of State, Sudan 2011 OSAC Crime and Security Report: Juba, 2011. (Washington, DC: GPO, 2011).

as the oil pipeline heads north from Juba to the oil fields, it must pass one last gauntlet of essentially ungoverned territory.

U.S. AFRICOM MUST ACT

There are three primary reasons why U.S. AFRICOM must assist Kenya and South Sudan in securing the oil pipeline. First, Kenya and South Sudan lack the capacity and capability to do so themselves. South Sudan's military has not had time to mature since independence and its military leaders have not developed a strategy to effectively prevent threats.[34] This results in uncoordinated response actions with no nesting of strategic and operational objectives. The South Sudanese are also confronted with a challenging operating environment. Much of the country contains extensive swamp areas and grassland regions. Severe altitude changes from high mountains further hinder South Sudanese security forces' ability to maneuver throughout the countryside. Finally, South Sudanese forces experience massive corruption of military members and poor resources which translates into an ineffective force.[35] These cumulative effects make the South Sudanese forces ineffective in their ability to provide security during the construction and eventual operation of the oil pipeline.

Though Kenya's military is more developed than South Sudan's, they continue to face many challenges. Kenya has spent years developing its capabilities and has become one of the strongest militaries in East Africa. Kenya possesses a diversified fleet of jets, tanks, weapons, and other types of military hardware to use in executing its security mission.

---

[34] Richard Rands, "In Need of Review: SPLA Transformation in 2006-10 and Beyond," Norwegian Ministry of Foreign Affairs, accessed on May 03, 2012, http://www.smallarmssurveysudan.org/pdfs/HSBA-SWP-23-SPLA-Transformation-2006-10-and-Beyond.pdf

[35] Department for International Development, Government of Canada, *The South Sudan Defense Forces in the Wake of the Juba Declaration, 2006.* Switzerland, 2006.

However, Kenyan forces are challenged by the country's geography and lack of infrastructure in remote areas to support these forces. Additionally, the Kenyan military has not been tested in this type of a security environment. Despite their superior military might, these weapons and planes do not translate to effective means by which to conduct asymmetric warfare. The Kenyans are new to oil pipeline security and would need significant guidance from others to successfully counter the asymmetric threats posed to oil pipelines.[36] It is going to be many years before either nation is prepared to assume primary responsibility for providing protection to the Lamu oil pipeline.

Second, there are numerous international and national organizations that are positioned to assist with promoting peace and security in East Africa, but not at the level required for oil pipeline security. The United Nations (UN), African Union (AU), and African Union Mission in Somalia (AMISOM) need to continue to work towards social, cultural, and government transformation to solve the problems that encourage terrorism and other violent extremist organizations. They should not be involved in developing training, techniques, and procedures (TTP) for oil pipeline security. Elements within U.S. AFRICOM however are perfectly suited to conduct this mission. It has the resources, knowledge, experience, and expertise to better serve South Sudanese and Kenyan forces in the best way to institute security measures along the pipeline.

Third, with construction of the oil pipeline scheduled to begin soon, U.S. AFRICOM must act without delay to minimize the opportunities terrorists, rebel groups, and militia have to derail the economic benefits the LAPSSET project is expected produce. The LAPSSET

---

[36] Army (Kenya), Army, Jane's, last modified 2009, http://articles.janes.com/articles/Janes-Sentinel-Security-Assessment-Central-Africa/Army-Kenya.html

project is projected to enhance the livelihood of more than 167 million Africans living in the region by providing them with increased job opportunities and a better quality of life.[37] For example in Kenya, the project is expected to more than double its gross domestic product.[38] This boost in revenue will enable Kenya to spend the money on a variety of social programs and economic enhancements for its citizens that will transform Kenyan society for the better. U.S. AFRICOM must not be complacent in thinking it's somebody else's problem or that the threat is minimal. This mentality would be a grave misinterpretation of the facts.

COUNTER-ARGUMENTS AND REBUTTAL

Some may argue that because Kenyan and South Sudanese forces face challenges pertaining to resources, capabilities, and inexperience, U.S. AFRICOM should focus their efforts to work with these forces on a broad level rather than specific to oil pipeline security. They would argue that each nation faces a multitude of threats that stretch their personnel and resources to the limit. These constraints in turn limit each nation's ability to freely reposition their forces as needed. For example, South Sudan is on the verge of fighting a large scale conventional war with Sudan. If war is declared, the South Sudanese will need to maximize every soldier, jet, and weapon in their inventory to protect their sovereignty. Kenya too is faced with competing demands. Their army and air force are currently engaged in Somalia fighting Al-Shabaab and their navy is busy combatting maritime piracy along the Kenyan coast. For both nations, these emergent threats limit their flexibility to shift resources and compels them to accept greater risk in other locations. A solution to this

---

[37] Kenya, Ethiopia, South Sudan Leaders Launch Lamu Port Construction, APA News, last accessed on May 4, 2012, http://www.apanews.net/photo/en/photo.php?id=169547

[38] James Anyanzwa, Juba Adds Fuel to Lamu Project, The Standard, last modified February 27, 2012, http://www.standardmedia.co.ke/business/InsidePage.php?id=2000052955&cid=14&story=Juba%20adds%20fuel%20to%20Lamu%20project

problem would be to hire out security along the oil pipeline while their militaries fight the broader the threats.

Others may argue that U.S. AFRICOM must encourage the UN, AU, and other African conscious organizations to take more of an active role in security functions. They may say that by assuming this responsibility, U.S. AFRICOM is enabling these groups to not engage fully as they should. By putting U.S. AFRICOM in the front on this issue, it opens the United States up to potentially make this an American problem rather than an African one. This would be counter to helping Africans provide solutions to African problems.

With all things considered, it is in the best interest of U.S. AFRICOM to lead security efforts for the Lamu oil pipeline. There is no disputing the fact that this mission would add strain and tension to already thinned Kenyan and South Sudanese forces. However, U.S. AFRICOM can work with both nations and leverage its relationships with international and national organizations to recommend creative solutions to better allocate their scare resources to achieve maximum efficiency. Contracting out security is not a prudent decision at this time. In Kenya, a police spokesman stated that "Kenya's private security industry is undergoing radical changes . . . the firms are struggling to meet new demands that seek to align their operations with those of government security agencies."[39] Given this disconnect between private security and the Kenyan government, which has a huge stake in the Lamu oil pipeline, now is not the time to try and establish agreement on this most critical issue. There are ways in which not to Americanize the mission and be able to give legitimate credit to Africans for developing solutions to their problems.

---

[39] Matt, "Kenya: The Government Teams Up with PSC's For Counter-Terrorism Efforts," *Feral Jundi Blog, accessed on May 4, 2012,* http://feraljundi.com/4237/kenya-the-government-teams-up-with-pscs-for-counter-terrorism-efforts/

RECOMMENDATIONS WITH LESSONS LEARNED

The following recommendations should be implemented in order to build security measures along the Lamu oil pipeline. Other than the first recommendation, all actions should be conducted simultaneously and as soon as possible.

First, this must be a coordinated effort between U.S. AFRICOM, Kenya, and South Sudan. Ethiopia's participation should be encouraged as they have a vital link in the LAPSSET project also. Once participation is agreed to, a thorough Strength-Weakness-Opportunity-Threat (SWOT) analysis should be conducted. This study will provide a starting point from where to begin to develop solutions to the security problem. U.S. AFRICOM would serve as lead for the SWOT analysis and receive input from the partner nations.

Second, U.S. AFRICOM must continue to encourage the UN and AU to apply maximum pressure on the governments of Sudan and South Sudan to cease their conflict. It will be very difficult to free South Sudanese forces for oil pipeline security duty with the continuous threat of major war against Sudan. Similarly, U.S. AFRICOM must continue to work with the global community to address the threat of Al-Shabaab. This will require a continued international commitment to rid East Africa of this threat. A key opportunity exists in the summer of 2012 when the Transitional Federal Government (TFG) in Somalia relinquishes power. U.S. AFRICOM must work with the UN, AU, and others to ensure a stable government is put in place to bring Somalia out of ruin. The results of these actions could equate to a lesser presence or complete withdrawal of Kenyan forces from Somalia. If so, parts of these forces could be reallocated along the oil pipeline for security measures.

Third, U.S. AFRICOM should use American Special Operations Forces (SOF) to conduct foreign internal defense (FID) in Kenya and South Sudan.[40] SOF forces could train the armies of South Sudan and Kenya on the proper TTP on how best to provide security to the oil pipeline. Training topics could include intelligence collection techniques, small unit tactical skills, communications, quick response actions, and reconnaissance procedures.[41] Recognizing the gap in proficiency that Kenyan and South Sudanese forces currently possess in these areas, SOF would be able to train their forces to an acceptable level of competence to effectively carry out these missions in a safe and effective manner. Moreover, SOF could work with both nations to identify strategic points of interest along the pipeline that would be most vulnerable to attack. Understanding that 100% security along the pipeline will never be achieved, this smart allocation of personnel would maximize deterrence and response capability along the pipeline.

Finally, U.S. AFRICOM should increase the resource allotment of these two nations. One capability action could be for the United States to sell helicopters to each nation. The U.S. has a history of selling used American equipment to allied nations who might not otherwise be able to fully fund the procurement of these items by themselves. Helicopters would enable the Kenyans and South Sudanese to gather intelligence and reconnaissance to help prevent an attack from happening. Helicopters would also be valuable assets for quickly moving from one area of the pipeline to another given the geographic challenges previously

---

[40] Per Joint Publication 3-22 dated July 12, 2010, Foreign Internal Defense (FID) is the participation by civilian and military agencies of a government in any of the action programs taken by another government . . .to free and protect its society from subversion, lawlessness, insurgency, terrorism, and other threats to their security.
[41] Brian Finlay, Johan Bergenas, and Veronica Tessler, Beyond Boundaries in Eastern Africa: Bridging the Security/Development Divide with International Security Assistance, The Stanley Foundation, last modified March 2011, http://www.stanleyfoundation.org/resources.cfm?type=policy

mentioned. U.S. AFRICOM should also be ready to support each nation by helping build helicopter storage and maintenance facilities at strategic points located along the pipeline. A challenge to this plan would be training Kenyan and South Sudanese forces in maintenance procedures of the helicopters as well as ensuring both nations had money available to pay for the upkeep of these assets. The second capability action would be for U.S. AFRICOM to develop an agreement between the nations to utilize unmanned aerial vehicles (UAV). These UAVs are perfectly suited to fly reconnaissance missions to identify potential attacks.

These recommendations have been previously implemented with great success (with the exception of the use of UAVs). In fact, U.S. Special Forces did a very similar mission in Colombia during the mid-2000s to train and equip Colombia's security forces to protect the Cano Limon oil pipeline. Per the United States Government Accountability Office report 05-971, the program experienced great success and provided lessons learned that can be applied to the Lamu oil pipeline.[42] Sending a small footprint of U.S. Special Forces to do this mission is cost effective and would allow for strategic communication opportunities to put African faces to these African problems.

CONCLUSION

The Lamu oil pipeline is a critical element of the LAPSSET project. The economic potential of East Africa lies in the security of the pipeline. An economically viable East Africa that provides for its citizens and enables them to live in peace and without fear decreases the motivation for disenfranchised youth to join terrorist groups, rebel groups, and armed militia. This in turn lessens the viability of these groups to carry out attacks. This will

---

[42] U.S. Government Accountability Office (GAO), *Security Assistance: Efforts to Secure Colombia's Cano Limon-Covenas Oil Pipeline Have Reduces Attacks, But Challenges Remain, 2005 (Washington, DC: GPO, 2005)*, 6.

make East Africa a safer place to live and indirectly lower the threats to America that originate in East Africa. U.S. AFRICOM's leadership and guidance to enhance partner nation capacity and capability to maximize security along the Lamu oil pipeline is in the best interest of U.S. AFRICOM and will unquestionably help Africans provide solutions to African problems.

Bibliography

Abdi, Mustafa. "Al-Shabaab." *New York Times*, October 17, 2011. http://topics.nytimes.com/top/reference/timestopics/organizations/s/al-shabab/index.html.

African Leaders Launch "Super Port" Project, Al Jazeera. Last modified March 2, 2012. http://www.aljazeera.com/news/africa/2012/03/20123283443196129.html.

Ali Gadkarim, Hassan. "Oil, Peace and Development: The Sudanese Impasse." Chr. Michelsen Institute. Last modified 2010. http://www.cmi.no/publications/file/3793-oil-peace-and-development-the-sudanese-impasse.pdf

Anderson, David and Michael Mihalka. "Is the Sky Falling? Energy Security and Transnational Terrorism." Center for Contemporary Conflict.

Anyanzwa, James. "Juba Adds Fuel to Lamu Project." The Standard. Last modified February 27, 2012. http://www.standardmedia.co.ke/business/InsidePage.php?id=2000052955&cid=14&story=Juba%20adds%fuel%20to%Lamu%20project.

Army (Kenya), Army. Jane's. Last modified 2009. http://articles.janes.com/articles/Janes-Sentinel-SecurityAssessment-Central-Africa/Army-Kenya.html.

Coble, Breane. "Shell's Corporate Social Responsibility in the Niger Delta." Last modified June 1, 2007. http://www.richmond.ac.uk/cms/pdfs/CobleBrief.pdf

Colombia's Cano Limon Pipeline Shut down after New Rebel Attack. Fox Business. Last modified March 20, 2012. http://www.foxbusiness.com/news/2012/03/20/colombias-cano-limon-pipeline-shut-down-after-new-rebel-attack/

Department for International Development, Government of Canada. *The South Sudan Defense Forces in the Wake of the Juba Declaration, 2006.* Switzerland, 2006.

Finlay, Brian, Johan Bergenas, and Veronica Tessler. "Beyond Boundaries in Eastern Africa: Bridging the Security/Development Divide with International Security Assistance." The Stanley Foundation. Last modified March 2011. http://www.stanleyfoundation.org/resources.cfm?type=policy.

Food and Medical Aid for 73,000 People. Malteser International. Last modified April 11, 2012. http://www.malteser-international.org/en/home/where-we-help/africa/kenya/relief-reconstruction rehabilitations/food-and-medical-aid-for-73000-people.html.

Herridge, Catherine. "Deadly Attacks Show Al-Shabaab Expanding Its Reach, With Potential for US Targets." Fox News. Last modified October 24, 2011, http://www.foxnews.com/world/2011/10/24/deadly-attacks-show-al-shabaab-expanding-its-reach-with-potential-for-us/.

Huge Lamu Port Project Launched for South Sudan and Ethiopia. Word Press. Last modified March 11, 2012. http://seeker401.wordpress.com/2012/03/11/massive-lamu-port-project-launched-for-south-sudan-and-ethiopia/.

Johnson, Reed. "6 Pipelines Blown Up In Mexico." *LA Times*, September 11, 2007. http://articles.latimes.com/2007/sep/11/world/fg-pipelines11.

Kambere, Geoffrey B. "Countering Al-Shabaab: A Case to Minimize Transnational Terrorist Threats Against Uganda." Master of Science thesis, Naval Post Graduate School, 2011. DTIC (ADA 556426).

Kenya, Ethiopia, South Sudan Leaders Launch Lamu Port Construction. APA News. Last accessed on May 4, 2012. http://www.apanews.net/photo/en/photo.php?id=169547.

Kenyan Troops Kill 60 Al-Shabaab Fighters in Somalia. BBC News Africa. Last modified January 7, 2012. http://www.bbc.co.uk/news/world-africa-16455039.

Lamu Port Project Launched for South Sudan and Ethiopia, British Broadcasting Corporation (BBC) News Africa. Last modified March 2, 2012. http://www.bbc.co.uk/news/world-africa-17231889.

LAPSSET Corridor and New Lamu Port Feasibility Study and Master Plans Report-Volume Three: LAPSSET Corridor Master Plan and Development Plan. Last modified May 2011. http://www.nigrizia.it/public/PDF%20e%20DOCUMENTI/lapsset-executive-summary.pdf

Matt. "Kenya: The Government Teams Up with PSC's For Counter-Terrorism Efforts." *Feral Jundi Blog.* Accessed on May 4, 2012. http://feraljundi.com/4237/kenya-the-government-teams-up-with-pscs-for-counter-terrorism-efforts/

Mayedu, Dennis. "Lamu Port and LAPSSET Construction Project Commenced." Open Book. Last modified March 10, 2012. http://www.openbook.co.ke/2012/lamu-port-and-lapsset-construction-project-commenced.html.

Nielsen, Ole. "Splitting Sudan Oil." *Nielsen Blog.* November 16, 2010. http://my.opera.com/nielsol/blog/2010/11/16/splitting-sudan-and-oil.

Pedersen, Jens. "South Sudan: Nation Building through a Pipeline?" Michelsen Institute. Last modified April 2012. http://www.cmi.no/sudan/resources.cfm?id=918-south-sudan-nationbuilding-through-a-pipeline.

Rands, Richard. "In Need of Review: SPLA Transformation in 2006-10 and Beyond." Norwegian Ministry of Foreign Affairs. Accessed on May 03, 2012. http://www.smallarmssurveysudan.org/pdfs/HSBA-SWP-23-SPLA-Transformation-2006-10-and-Beyond.pdf

Rapier, Robert. "Oil Infrastructure and Terrorism Part II." Consumer Energy Report. Last modified October 6, 2010. http://www.consumerenergyreport.com/2010/10/06/oil-infrastructure-and-terrorism-part-ii.

Simonse, Simon. Human Security in the Borderlands of Sudan, Uganda, and Kenya. IKV Pax Christi. Last modified July 2011. http://www.ikvpaxchristi.nl/UK/above_publications.htm.

South Sudan's Rebel Groups Threatened to Prevent the Construction of New Oil Pipeline; Warned "Theaters of War". South Sudan News Agency. Last modified January 25, 2012. http://www.southsudannewsagency.com/news/press-releases/south-sudans-rebel-groups-threatened-to-prevent-the-construction-of-new-oil-pipeline-warned-theaters-of-war.

South Sudan to Withdraw Troops from Heglig Oil Field. BBC News Africa. Last modified April 20, 2012. http://www.bbc.co.uk/news/world-africa-17787142.

The Failed States Index. Foreign Policy. Last modified June 22, 2009. http://www.foreignpolicy.com/articles2009/06/22/2009_failed_states_index_interactive_map_and_rankings.

U.S. Department of State. *Sudan 2011 OSAC Crime and Security Report: Juba, 2011.* Washington, DC: GPO, 2011.

U.S. Government Accountability Office (GAO). *Maritime Security, Federal Efforts Needed to Address Challenges in Preventing and Responding to Terrorist Attacks on Energy Commodity Tankers, 2007.* Washington, DC: GPO, 2007.

U.S. Government Accountability Office (GAO). *Security Assistance: Efforts to Secure Colombia's Cano Limon-Covenas Oil Pipeline Have Reduces Attacks, But Challenges Remain, 2005.* Washington, DC: GPO, 2005.